30-minute meals from WW

Seven C3

Produced by Seven Publishing Ltd on behalf of WW International, Inc. Published July 2019. All rights reserved. No part of this publication may be reproduced, stored in retrieval system or transmitted in any form by any means, electronic, mechanical photocopying, recording or otherwise, without the prior written permission of Seven Publishing Ltd. First published in Great Britain by Seven Publishing Ltd.

Seven Publishing Ltd,
3-7 Herbal Hill, London EC1R 5EJ
www.seven.co.uk

10 9 8 7 6 5 4 3 2 1

A CIP catalogue record for this book is available from the British Library.

ISBN: 978-1-9996673-6-8

WW PUBLISHING TEAM

Samantha Rees, Harriet Joy, Nicola Kirk, Jessica O'Shea

FOR SEVEN PUBLISHING LTD
FOOD

Food editor: Nadine Brown

Recipes: Nadine Brown, Jenna Leiter, Ella Tarn

EDITORIAL

Editor-in-chief: Helen Renshaw

Editor: Christine Faughlin

Sub-editor: Ward Hellewell

DESIGN & PHOTOGRAPHY

Art director: Liz Baird

Photographer: Dan Jones

Food stylists: Sarah Cook, Jenna Leiter, Ella Tarn

Prop stylist: Agathe Gits

ACCOUNT MANAGEMENT

Account manager: Gina Cavaciuti

Group publishing director: Kirsten Price

PRODUCTION

Print lead: Liz Knipe

Colour reproduction by F1 Colour

Printed in the UK by Pureprint

THE SMALL PRINT

Eggs We use medium eggs, unless otherwise stated. Pregnant women, the elderly and children should avoid recipes with eggs which are raw or not fully cooked if not produced under the British Lion code of practice.

Fruit and vegetables Recipes use medium-size fruit and veg, unless otherwise stated.

Reduced-fat soft cheese Where a recipe uses reduced-fat soft cheese, we mean a soft cheese with 30% less fat than its full-fat equivalent.

Low-fat spread When a recipe uses a low-fat spread, we mean a spread with a fat content of no more than 39%.

Microwaves If we have used a microwave in any of our recipes, the timings will be for an 850-watt microwave oven.

Prep and cook times These are approximate and meant to be guidelines only. Prep time includes all steps up to and following the main cooking time(s). Stated cook times may vary according to your oven.

Vegetarian Recipes displaying a vegetarian symbol include non-meat ingredients, but may also contain processed products that aren't always vegetarian, such as pesto. If you're a vegetarian, you should ensure you use vegetarian varieties and check the ingredients labels. Where we reference vegetarian **Italian-style hard cheese** in vegetarian recipes, we mean a cheese similar to Parmesan (which is not vegetarian) but which is suitable for vegetarians.

Vegan recipes displaying a vegan symbol include no products made from or with the aid of animals or animal products.

Gluten free Recipes that are labelled as gluten free include ingredients that naturally do not contain gluten, but they may also contain processed products, such as sauces, stock cubes and spice mixes. If so, you should ensure that those products do not include any gluten-containing ingredients (wheat, barley or rye) – these will be highlighted in the ingredients list on the product label. Manufacturers may also indicate whether there is a chance their product may have been accidentally contaminated with gluten during the manufacturing process. For more information and guidance on gluten-free products, visit www.coeliac.org.uk

Nut free Recipes displaying a nut free symbol include ingredients that do not contain nuts, but may include ingredients produced in facilities that also handle nut products. If you have a nut allergy, check ingredients labels for more information.

Dairy free Recipes displaying a dairy free symbol include ingredients that naturally do not contain dairy, but may include ingredients produced in facilities that also handle dairy products. If you have a dairy allergy, check ingredients labels for more information.

SmartPoints® have been calculated using the values for generic foods, not brands (except where stated). Tracking using branded items may affect the recorded SmartPoints.

WHEN YOU SEE THESE SYMBOLS:

0 Tells you the SmartPoints value per serving

 Indicates a recipe is gluten free

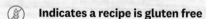 Indicates a recipe is vegetarian

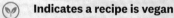 Indicates a recipe is vegan

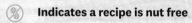 Indicates a recipe is nut free

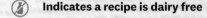 Indicates a recipe is dairy free

Contents

Meals in minutes

Fast food doesn't have to be unhealthy food, as this collection of more than 60 creative, delicious and simple recipes shows. From soups, salads, sandwiches and stir-fries to easy curries, speedy pastas and quick bakes, all the dishes in *30-minute meals from WW* are ready to eat in half an hour or under. Just the thing for those who'd rather spend more of their time enjoying a meal than cooking it…

Soups, salads & sandwiches

Seafood chowder topped with crispy breadcrumbs

serves 4   **prep time 10 minutes**   **cook time 20 minutes**

A rich soup that's packed with a medley of fish, mussels, prawns and squid, then finished with a scattering of tarragon and golden breadcrumbs.

2 slices WW Malted Danish Bread, roughly torn

1 tablespoon olive oil

1 large leek, trimmed and finely sliced

1 tablespoon plain flour

700ml fish stock, made with 1 stock cube

250ml semi-skimmed milk

300g fish pie mix

200g mixed seafood selection – we used a mix of mussels, king prawns and squid rings

Handful fresh tarragon, finely chopped

Lemon wedges, to serve

1   Preheat the oven to 200°C, fan 180°C, gas mark 6. Put the bread in a food processor and pulse until it forms crumbs. Add half the oil and pulse until combined. Season the crumbs, then spread on a baking tray and bake for 6-8 minutes, stirring once, until crisp and golden, then set aside.

2   Meanwhile, set a large pan over a medium-high heat and add the remaining oil. Cook the leek, stirring occasionally, for 5 minutes until softened, then stir in the flour and cook for a further 2 minutes.

3   Stir in the stock and bring the mixture to the boil. Reduce the heat and add the milk and fish pie mix. Bring to a simmer and cook for 3 minutes, then add the seafood mix and simmer for a final 2 minutes.

4   Stir in half the tarragon, season to taste, then ladle into bowls. Scatter over the breadcrumbs and remaining tarragon, then serve with the lemon wedges on the side.

 SmartPoints value per serving

Cook's tip
If you have more time, bulk out the dish by adding 400g halved new potatoes before adding the fish, and simmering for 15 minutes, for an extra 2 SmartPoints per serving.

Red pepper, prosciutto & mozzarella salad

serves 4   prep time 5 minutes

On the table in 5 minutes flat, this colourful salad is just the thing for those days where you simply haven't the time to cook.

80g rocket

3 roasted red peppers in brine, drained and cut into thick strips

2 x 125g balls light mozzarella, drained and torn

8 slices prosciutto, roughly torn

FOR THE SALAD DRESSING

3 x 15g sachets WW Balsamic Salad Dressing

1 teaspoon clear honey

1   Arrange the rocket on a serving platter and top with the red peppers, mozzarella and prosciutto.

2   In a small bowl, whisk together the salad dressing ingredients, then drizzle the dressing over the salad and serve seasoned with freshly ground black pepper.

6   **SmartPoints value per serving**

Greek-style lemon & chicken soup

serves 4   prep time 10 minutes   cook time 20 minutes

Looking for a warm-weather soup that's hearty yet fresh? Our take
on a classic lemon-infused Greek dish ticks all the boxes.

Calorie controlled cooking spray
1 small onion, finely diced
**1 litre hot chicken stock, made
with 2 stock cubes**
100g orzo pasta
**200g cooked skinless chicken
breast fillet, shredded**
3 eggs
Pared zest and juice of 2 lemons
80g young leaf spinach
20g fresh dill, fronds picked

1 Mist a large pan with cooking spray and fry the onion over a
medium-high heat for 5-6 minutes until softened.

2 Reserve 200ml of the stock, then add the remainder to the pan
and bring to the boil. Add the orzo, then reduce the heat and simmer
for 7 minutes until al dente. Stir in the chicken and cook for 2 minutes
until heated through.

3 Meanwhile, whisk the eggs in a large bowl for 2 minutes until frothy.
Slowly pour in the lemon juice while whisking, then very gradually
add the reserved stock, whisking constantly.

4 Pour the egg mixture into the soup and stir to combine. Cook for
2-3 minutes on a low heat until the soup is thickened. Stir in the
spinach and cook for 1 minute until wilted.

5 Ladle the soup into bowls, season to taste then serve garnished
with the dill and lemon zest.

Cook's tip
You could serve this with
a 60g wholemeal pitta bread
per person, for an extra
4 SmartPoints per serving.

3 SmartPoints value per serving

Mackerel, courgette, beetroot & white bean salad

serves 4   **prep time 10 minutes**

Tasty oil-rich mackerel, bright earthy beetroot and ZeroPoint cannellini beans come together to delicious effect in this super-speedy salad.

400g tin cannellini beans, drained and rinsed

2 courgettes, trimmed and peeled into ribbons using a vegetable peeler

3 x 80g smoked mackerel fillets, skin removed and discarded, and flesh broken into large flakes

2 cooked beetroots, cut into wedges

Pared zest of 2 lemons, to serve

FOR THE SALAD DRESSING

2 tablespoons extra-virgin olive oil

Juice of 2 lemons

Small handful of fresh flat-leaf parsley, roughly chopped

1   In a large bowl, combine the beans, courgette ribbons and mackerel.

2   To make the dressing, whisk the olive oil and lemon juice together in a small bowl, then whisk in the parsley and season to taste.

3   Pour the dressing over the salad and toss to coat. Add the beetroot and gently toss to combine, then scatter over the lemon zest and serve.

7   **SmartPoints value per serving**

Cook's tip
To reduce the SmartPoints to 2 per serving, use whole griddled sardines instead of the smoked mackerel.

Tabbouleh bowl with marinated prawns, tomatoes & feta

serves 4   **prep time 5 minutes + standing**

This popular bulgur wheat-based salad is transformed into a filling, flavoursome main thanks to the addition of juicy prawns, hot chilli flakes and salty feta.

200g bulgur wheat
Juice of 2 lemons
10g fresh mint, leaves picked and finely chopped
1½ tablespoons olive oil
¼ teaspoon chilli flakes
300g cooked and peeled king prawns
10 cherry tomatoes, quartered
80g light feta cheese, crumbled
30g rocket
1 large garlic clove, finely chopped

1   Put the bulgur wheat in a large heatproof bowl and cover with 350ml freshly boiled water. Season, then cover with clingfilm and set aside for 25 minutes until the bulgur wheat is tender, but still has some bite.

2   Meanwhile, in a bowl, whisk together half the lemon juice and mint with all the oil and chilli flakes. Add the prawns, then stir and set aside to marinate for 20 minutes at room temperature.

3   Drain off any excess liquid from the bulgur wheat. Stir in the tomatoes, feta, rocket, garlic and remaining mint and lemon juice, then season to taste.

4   Divide the tabbouleh between bowls, then top with the prawns and drizzle over the marinade to serve.

7   **SmartPoints value per serving**

Spiced carrot & ginger soup

serves 4   prep time 5 minutes   cook time 25 minutes   freezable

Sweet carrots and fiery root ginger are a match made in soup heaven. We've made this dish even more delicious with a hint of harissa and a trio of chopped fresh herbs.

Calorie controlled cooking spray

30g fresh ginger, grated

2 cloves garlic, finely chopped

1 tablespoon harissa paste

1 teaspoon ground cumin

½ teaspoon ground coriander

2 x 300g packs prepared carrot batons

900ml vegetable stock, made with 1 stock cube

Small handful each fresh coriander, flat-leaf parsley and mint, leaves picked and roughly chopped

Mixed salad leaves, to serve

1   Mist a large pan with cooking spray and cook the ginger and garlic over a medium heat for 2 minutes until softened. Add the harissa and spices and cook for 1 minute until fragrant. Add the carrots and stir to combine.

2   Pour in the stock and bring to the boil. Reduce the heat, then simmer, covered, for 20 minutes until the carrots are just tender.

3   Using a stick blender, blitz the soup until completely smooth. Ladle into bowls, scatter over the fresh herbs, season with freshly ground black pepper and serve with the salad leaves on the side.

The soup can be frozen in an airtight container for up to 3 months.

0   SmartPoints value per serving

Giant couscous bowl with chicken & homemade cashew pesto

serves 4   prep time 15 minutes   cook time 10 minutes

An easy meal-in-a-bowl made extra special with a generous spoonful of punchy, homemade cashew and basil pesto.

240g wholewheat giant couscous
50g fresh basil, leaves picked
40g unsalted raw cashew nuts
1 garlic clove, roughly chopped
40g Parmesan, finely grated
1½ tablespoons olive oil
10 cherry tomatoes, halved
Pared zest and juice of ½ lemon
200g cooked skinless chicken breast fillet, sliced

1   Bring a large pan of water to the boil, add the couscous and cook for 8 minutes until tender. Drain, cool under cold running water, then drain again. Set aside.

2   Meanwhile, put 40g of the basil in a mini food processor with the cashews and garlic, then pulse until combined. Add the Parmesan and process to a coarse purée. With the motor still running, gradually add the oil, followed by 50ml water, until the mixture reaches a pesto-like consistency. Season to taste and set aside.

3   Thinly slice the remaining basil and add it to the drained couscous along with the tomatoes and lemon zest and juice. Toss to combine.

4   Divide the couscous between bowls and top with the chicken. Spoon over the cashew pesto then serve seasoned with freshly ground black pepper.

 **12**   SmartPoints value per serving

Red lentil & chorizo soup

serves 4   **prep time 5 minutes**   **cook time 25 minutes**   **freezable**

Hearty red lentils, spicy chorizo, fragrant smoked paprika... this trio of tasty Spanish ingredients is the hero of this filling soup that's perfect for weeknight suppers.

Calorie controlled cooking spray

100g diced chorizo

1 onion, finely diced

2 garlic cloves, finely chopped

1 teaspoon smoked paprika

½ teaspoon cumin seeds

180g dried red lentils, rinsed

400g tin chopped tomatoes

750ml vegetable stock, made with 1 stock cube

Small handful fresh flat-leaf parsley, roughly chopped, to serve

1 Mist a large pan with cooking spray and set over a medium-high heat. Add the chorizo and cook for 2 minutes until it has released its oil and turned crisp. Transfer to a bowl with a slotted spoon, leaving the oil in the pan.

2 Add the onion, garlic and spices to the pan and cook for 5 minutes until the onion has started to soften.

3 Add the lentils and stir to coat, then add the tomatoes and stock. Bring to the boil, then reduce the heat and simmer, covered, for 15 minutes, until the lentils are tender.

4 Remove the lid and stir the chorizo back into the soup, then ladle into bowls and scatter over the chopped parsley to serve.

The soup can be frozen in an airtight container for up to 3 months.

 SmartPoints value per serving

Cook's tip
Make this veggie by leaving out the chorizo and stirring 3 Linda McCartney Chorizo and Red Pepper Sausages (cooked to pack instructions and chopped) into the soup before serving. The SmartPoints will be 2 per serving.

Mexican bean wraps

makes 4   prep time 5 minutes   cook time 25 minutes   freezable

A spicy combo of ZeroPoint beans – including red kidney, pinto, cannellini, borlotti and black eyed – makes for a deliciously filling lunch.

Calorie controlled cooking spray

1 small white onion, thinly sliced

2 garlic cloves, finely chopped

¼ teaspoon chilli flakes

3 tomatoes, roughly chopped

2 tablespoons balsamic vinegar

400g tin mixed beans in water, drained and rinsed

4 WW Wholemeal Wraps

2 tablespoons reduced-fat soured cream

80g iceberg lettuce, torn

60g WW Reduced Fat Grated Mature Cheese

1   Mist a large pan with cooking spray and cook the onion over a medium heat for 6-8 minutes until softened. Add the garlic and cook for 1 minute.

2   Add the chilli flakes and cook for a further minute, then stir in the tomatoes and vinegar and season well. Cover and cook for 5 minutes until the tomatoes have just started to break down, then stir in the beans and simmer for 10 minutes until the sauce is reduced and thickened.

3   Meanwhile, heat the wraps to pack instructions. Spread them with the soured cream, then top with the lettuce, bean chilli and cheese. Roll up and serve.

The chilli can be frozen in an airtight container for up to 3 months.

5   SmartPoints value per wrap

Cauliflower & Stilton soup

serves 4   **prep time 10 minutes**   **cook time 20 minutes**   **freezable**

Looking for an update on broccoli and Stilton soup? This warming veggie dish uses cauliflower florets for a satisfying, creamy texture and subtle flavour.

Calorie controlled cooking spray

2 shallots, roughly chopped

1 teaspoon dried oregano

1 cauliflower, trimmed and cut into small florets

900ml vegetable stock, made with 1 stock cube

80g Stilton, crumbled

Small handful fresh flat-leaf parsley, roughly chopped

4 x 22g slices calorie controlled brown bread

1   Mist a large pan with cooking spray and fry the shallots over a medium-high heat for 5 minutes until starting to soften. Add the oregano and cook for a further minute.

2   Add the cauliflower and stock, then cover and bring to the boil. Reduce the heat and simmer for 15 minutes until the cauliflower is tender.

3   Transfer half of the cauliflower to a bowl using a slotted spoon, and set aside. Add half the Stilton to the soup, then use a stick blender to blitz until smooth. Season to taste.

4   Put the reserved cauliflower back into the soup with most of the parsley. Divide between bowls and scatter over the remaining Stilton and parsley. Season with freshly ground black pepper, then toast the bread and serve alongside the soup.

The soup can be frozen in an airtight container for up to 3 months.

⑤   SmartPoints value per serving

Cook's tip

Shallots can be tricky to peel. If you have time, soak them in hot water for 1-2 minutes first – it softens the skin, making it easier to take off.

Open sandwiches

Lightly toasted sourdough piled high with the right combination of healthier ingredients can transform the humble lunchtime sandwich into something memorable.

Chicken, cress & aïoli
makes 2
prep time 10 minutes

To make the aïoli, combine 40g **reduced-fat mayonnaise**, the juice of ½ **lemon** and 1 finely chopped **garlic clove** in a small bowl, and season to taste. Lightly toast 2 x 50g slices **sourdough bread** and spread with a little of the aïoli. Top with 60g shredded **cooked skinless chicken breast fillet** and 20g **cress**, then spoon over the remaining aïoli and scatter over the pared zest of ½ **lemon**. Serve seasoned with **freshly ground black pepper**.

 6   SmartPoints value per open sandwich

Tuna Niçoise
makes 2
prep time 10 minutes cook time 10 minutes

Bring a small pan of water to the boil, then reduce to a simmer. Carefully lower 1 **egg** into the water and cook, uncovered, for 8 minutes. Transfer the egg to a bowl of iced water and leave for 2 minutes to cool, then peel, cut in half and set aside. While the egg is boiling, thinly slice ¼ **red onion**, combine with 1 tablespoon **red wine vinegar** and a pinch of salt in a small bowl, then set aside for 10 minutes. Drain and finely chop 2 **anchovy fillets**, reserving 1 tablespoon of the **anchovy oil**. Combine the reserved anchovy oil with ½ teaspoon **Dijon mustard**, then stir the mixture together with the chopped anchovies and a 160g tin drained **tuna in spring water**. Lightly toast 2 x 50g slices **sourdough bread**, then top with some **salad leaves**, the tuna mixture, the egg and 4 sliced pitted **black olives**. Serve seasoned with **freshly ground black pepper**.

 6   SmartPoints value per open sandwich

Halloumi, beetroot & broad beans
makes 2
prep time 15 minutes cook time 10 minutes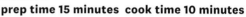

Cook 130g frozen **broad beans** in a pan of boiling water for 3 minutes, then drain and refresh under cold running water. Peel off the outer skins and discard, then set aside 1 tablespoon of the beans. Put the rest into a mini food processor with 3 tablespoons **lemon juice**, 1 tablespoon chopped **fresh mint** and 1 small chopped **garlic clove**. Blitz to a purée, then season to taste and set aside. Mist a large nonstick pan with **calorie controlled cooking spray**, then fry 4 x 20g slices **light halloumi** over a medium heat for 2 minutes on each side. Set aside. Lightly toast 2 x 50g slices **sourdough bread**, then spread with the bean purée. Top with the halloumi and 1 small **cooked beetroot**, cut into wedges, then scatter over the reserved broad beans and some extra mint. Serve seasoned with **freshly ground black pepper**.

 7   SmartPoints value per open sandwich

Crab, radish & lime
makes 2
prep time 5 minutes

Combine a 170g tin drained **crab in brine** with 1 tablespoon **fat-free natural yogurt**, 1 tablespoon chopped **fresh coriander** and the juice of ½ **lime** in a bowl, and season to taste. Lightly toast 2 x 50g slices **sourdough bread** and top with the crab mixture. Scatter over 1 small trimmed and thinly sliced **radish** and some more chopped fresh coriander, then serve seasoned with **freshly ground black pepper**.

 4   SmartPoints value per open sandwich

Pan-fries
& stir-fries

Steak & white bean mash with mushroom sauce

serves 4   prep time 5 minutes   cook time 20 minutes

Succulent sirloin steaks served with a creamy bean mash, mushroom sauce and steamed green beans – ideal for when you're looking for something speedy but special.

Calorie controlled cooking spray

4 x 225g sirloin steaks, fat trimmed

200g chestnut mushrooms, sliced

4 garlic cloves, crushed

2 tablespoons wholegrain mustard, plus an extra 2 teaspoons

250ml chicken stock, made with 1 stock cube

100g half-fat crème fraîche

Finely grated zest and juice of ½ lemon

3 x 400g tins cannellini beans, drained and rinsed

Large handful fresh flat-leaf parsley, roughly chopped

200g fine green beans

1 Mist a very large nonstick frying pan with cooking spray and fry the steaks over a high heat for 3 minutes on each side, or until cooked to your liking. Transfer to a plate, cover loosely with kitchen foil and set aside to rest.

2 Add the mushrooms to the pan and stir-fry for 5-6 minutes until golden, then add a quarter of the garlic and 2 tablespoons mustard and cook for another minute. Stir in 150ml of the stock and all the crème fraîche, then add the lemon juice and season to taste with freshly ground black pepper. Keep warm over a low heat.

3 Meanwhile, mist a large nonstick pan with cooking spray and cook the remaining garlic over a medium heat for 1 minute. Stir in the cannellini beans and the remaining stock and cook for 2-3 minutes until heated through. Stir in the parsley, lemon zest and the remaining wholegrain mustard, season to taste and roughly mash with a potato masher.

4 Cook the green beans in a pan of boiling water for 4-5 minutes until tender, then drain.

5 Divide the mash and beans between plates, top the mash with the steaks and serve with the mushroom sauce spooned over.

Cook's tip
For the mash, you could also use butterbeans or chickpeas, or a mixture of both, for no extra SmartPoints.

8 SmartPoints value per serving

Turkey quesadillas

serves 4   prep time 10 minutes   cook time 20 minutes

The ultimate one-pan comfort food that's perfect for lunch, dinner or a late-night snack. If you like things spicy, add a bit of chilli powder to the spice mix for no extra SmartPoints.

350g turkey breast strips
1½ teaspoons dried thyme
1½ teaspoons ground allspice
1½ teaspoons ground paprika
Calorie controlled cooking spray
1 onion, thinly sliced
1 green pepper, deseeded and thinly sliced
1 red pepper, deseeded and thinly sliced
4 large white tortilla wraps
120g WW Reduced Fat Grated Mature Cheese
Mixed salad leaves, to serve
Lime wedges, to serve

1   Put the turkey, thyme, allspice and paprika in a bowl, season, then mix to combine and set aside.

2   Mist a large nonstick frying pan with cooking spray and cook the onion and peppers over a medium heat for 5 minutes until starting to soften. Add the turkey and cook for another 5-7 minutes until cooked through and golden. Transfer to a plate and wipe the pan clean with kitchen paper.

3   Mist the pan with more cooking spray. Put 1 tortilla wrap into the pan, scatter over a quarter of the cheese, then half the turkey mixture and another quarter of the cheese. Top with a second tortilla wrap. Cook for 2 minutes, pressing down on the tortilla with a spatula, then gently turn and cook on the other side for a final 2 minutes. Slide out of the pan, then repeat with the remaining tortillas, cheese and turkey mixture.

4   Cut each quesadilla in half and then cut each half into three wedges. Serve with the salad leaves and lime wedges on the side.

 8   Points value per serving

Cook's tip
Use chicken breast strips instead of turkey for no extra SmartPoints. Save even more time by using 1 tablespoon fajita spice mix instead of the thyme, allspice and paprika.

Green shakshuka

serves 4   prep time 10 minutes   cook time 20 minutes

Skip the lengthy brunch queues at your local cafe, and whip up this lean, green egg bake instead. It's a fresh new take on the traditional tomato-based version.

Calorie controlled cooking spray

3 large leeks, trimmed and thinly sliced

2 garlic cloves, finely chopped

2 teaspoons cumin seeds

1 teaspoon ground coriander

1 tablespoon harissa paste

300g frozen peas

500g frozen spinach

2 tablespoons finely chopped fresh mint, plus extra to serve

2 tablespoons finely chopped fresh coriander, plus extra to serve

4 large eggs

100g light feta

1 small red chilli, deseeded and finely sliced

1 Mist a large lidded frying pan with cooking spray and cook the leeks, stirring, over a medium heat for 3-4 minutes until they start to soften. Add the garlic, cumin seeds and ground coriander, and cook for another minute. Stir in the harissa, peas and spinach, then cover and cook for 5 minutes, stirring occasionally.

2 Stir in the fresh herbs and season to taste. Using a spoon, create four wells in the mixture. Crack an egg into each well, then cover and cook for 5-7 minutes until the egg whites are set and the yolks soft.

3 Crumble over the feta and scatter over the chilli to serve.

2 SmartPoints value per serving

Cook's tip
Serve this with 4 x 65g flatbreads for a total of 7 SmartPoints per serving.

Sea bass with salsa verde

serves 4   **prep time 10 minutes**   **cook time 15 minutes**

Add a bit of oomph to pan-fried fish with a generous helping of boldly flavoured salsa verde. You can also serve this salsa verde with griddled chicken, pork or vegetables.

750g baby new potatoes, larger ones halved

½ tablespoon extra-virgin olive oil

1 tablespoon chopped fresh mint

4 x 90g sea bass fillets

Calorie controlled cooking spray

80g mixed salad leaves

150g cherry tomatoes, quartered

2 teaspoons balsamic vinegar

Lemon wedges, to serve

FOR THE SALSA VERDE

3 anchovies in oil, drained and roughly chopped

1 tablespoon capers, drained and rinsed

1 tablespoon freshly squeezed lemon juice

½ small garlic clove, crushed

3 tablespoons chopped fresh flat-leaf parsley

2 tablespoons chopped fresh basil

2 tablespoons extra-virgin olive oil

1 Cook the potatoes in a large pan of boiling water for 12-15 minutes until tender, then drain and roughly crush with a potato masher. Toss with the oil and mint.

2 Meanwhile, make the salsa verde. Put all the ingredients except the oil into a mini food processor, and blitz to a coarse purée. Stir in the oil, season to taste, then set aside. If you don't have a mini food processor, you can chop everything finely by hand.

3 Make 3 shallow slashes through the skin of each fish fillet. Mist a large nonstick frying pan with cooking spray and cook the fish, skin-side down, over a medium heat for 2-3 minutes. Gently turn and cook for another 1-2 minutes, until just cooked through.

4 In a bowl, combine the salad leaves and tomatoes, then drizzle over the balsamic vinegar. Divide the salad, crushed potatoes and sea bass between plates. Spoon over the salsa verde and serve with the lemon wedges.

7   **SmartPoints value per serving**

Cook's tip

Remove the anchovies from the salsa if you don't like them. The SmartPoints will remain the same.

Quorn tacos with red cabbage slaw

serves 4   **prep time 5 minutes**   **cook time 15 minutes**

Put a smoky spin on a Mexican favourite by adding chipotle marinade to a veggie taco mix.
If you have any leftover slaw, serve it on the side or save it for lunch the next day.

Calorie controlled cooking spray
1 small onion, finely chopped
1 garlic clove, finely chopped
¼ tablespoon chilli flakes
250g frozen Quorn mince
2 x 50g sachets WW Smoky Chipotle Marinade
1 teaspoon tomato purée
8 taco shells
60g iceberg lettuce, shredded
Lime wedges, to serve

FOR THE RED CABBAGE SLAW
75g reduced-fat mayonnaise
50g 0% fat natural Greek yogurt
1 tablespoon white wine vinegar
Juice of ½ lime
300g red cabbage, shredded
1 carrot, coarsely grated
2 spring onions, trimmed and sliced

1   Mist a large nonstick pan with cooking spray and fry the onion, garlic and chilli flakes over a medium heat for 4-5 minutes until starting to soften.

2   Add the Quorn mince, breaking up any large lumps with a wooden spoon. Stir in the chipotle marinade and tomato purée, along with 100ml water. Season to taste, then cover and simmer for 10 minutes, until the Quorn is cooked through.

3   Meanwhile, make the slaw. Combine the mayonnaise, yogurt, white wine vinegar and lime juice in a large bowl. Add the cabbage, carrot and spring onions and stir to combine. Season to taste.

4   Heat the taco shells to pack instructions, then fill with the lettuce leaves, Quorn and slaw. Serve with the lime wedges on the side.

   SmartPoints value per serving

Cook's tip
You could serve this with
4 WW Wraps instead of the
taco shells – the SmartPoints
will be the same.

Stir-fried beef with oyster sauce

serves 4   **prep time 5 minutes**   **cook time 15 minutes**

Toss lean beef strips in a wok with broccoli, oyster mushrooms, fresh egg noodles and a savoury sauce to make this Chinese classic.

Calorie controlled cooking spray

300g lean beef stir-fry strips

200g Tenderstem broccoli, trimmed and cut into bite-size pieces

1 onion, thinly sliced

250g oyster mushrooms, halved if large

2 garlic cloves, thinly sliced

100ml oyster sauce

400g fresh egg noodles (we used Morrisons)

1   Mist a large nonstick wok or frying pan with cooking spray and stir-fry the beef over a medium heat for 2 minutes, then remove from the wok and set aside on a plate.

2   Mist the wok with more cooking spray, then stir-fry the broccoli, onion and mushrooms for 4-5 minutes. Add the garlic and stir-fry for 2 minutes.

3   Return the beef to the wok along with the oyster sauce, then stir-fry for 1 minute, until combined. Add the noodles and stir-fry for 2 minutes, until heated through.

4   Divide between bowls and serve.

 SmartPoints value per serving

Miso & orange glazed salmon

serves 4 **prep time 5 minutes** **cook time 15 minutes**

When it comes to flavour, tender ZeroPoint salmon brushed with a Japanese-inspired orange and miso glaze is hard to beat. Serve it with a wild rice mix for a dish that looks great on the plate.

2 tablespoons white miso paste

½ tablespoon clear honey

Finely grated zest of ½ orange, plus 3 tablespoons juice

½ tablespoon mirin

4 x 130g skin-on salmon fillets

2 tablespoons pumpkin seeds

Calorie controlled cooking spray

2 teaspoons sesame seeds

½ tablespoon toasted sesame oil

100g young leaf spinach

2 x 250g pouches microwave long grain & wild rice

1 In a large bowl, combine the miso paste, honey, most of the orange zest, 2 tablespoons of the orange juice and the mirin, then add the salmon fillets and turn to coat. Set aside.

2 Set a large nonstick frying pan over a medium heat, add the pumpkin seeds and toast, stirring, until fragrant, then transfer to a bowl and set aside. Mist the pan with cooking spray and increase the heat to medium-high. Cook the salmon fillets, skin-side down, for 5 minutes, then carefully turn over and cook for 2-3 minutes until just cooked through. Remove from the heat and scatter over the sesame seeds.

3 In a small bowl, mix the remaining orange juice with the sesame oil, then toss with the spinach. Scatter over the toasted pumpkin seeds.

4 Cook the rice to pack instructions. Serve the salmon, spinach salad and rice garnished with the remaining orange zest.

 SmartPoints value per serving

Cook's tip

Instead of the rice, try serving this with 250g quinoa, cooked to pack instructions, for 9 SmartPoints per serving.

Rainbow vegetable stir-fry

serves 4   **prep time 10 minutes**   **cook time 10 minutes**

Sunshine in a bowl! Brightly coloured crunchy veg, wok-fried with a Mongolian-inspired sauce, is the perfect warm-weather vegan stir-fry.

60ml soy sauce

2 tablespoons sweet chilli sauce

1 tablespoon sriracha hot chilli sauce

2 tablespoons mirin

½ tablespoon cornflour

2 teaspoons vegetable oil

100g radishes, trimmed and quartered

1 red pepper, deseeded and thinly sliced

100g mangetout

100g baby corn, halved lengthways

2 pak choi, chopped

2 garlic cloves, crushed

3cm piece fresh ginger, grated

2 x 250g pouches wholegrain microwave rice

2 spring onions, trimmed and thinly sliced

Handful coriander leaves, to serve

1   In a small bowl, whisk together the soy, sweet chilli and sriracha sauces with the mirin and 60ml cold water. Put the cornflour in a separate small bowl and stir in enough of the sauce mixture to form a smooth paste. Mix the paste back into the remaining sauce mixture, then set aside.

2   Heat the oil in a large nonstick wok or frying pan set over a high heat. Stir-fry the vegetables for 3-4 minutes until just tender, then add the garlic and ginger and cook for another minute. Pour in the sauce mixture and stir-fry for 1-2 minutes until the sauce has thickened and all the vegetables are coated.

3   Microwave the rice to pack instructions and serve with the stir-fry garnished with the spring onions and coriander.

9   **SmartPoints value per serving**

Cook's tip
Use shredded cabbage instead of pak choi, if you prefer.

Pork chops with creamy leeks & new potatoes

serves 4   prep time 5 minutes   cook time 15 minutes

Make these pork chops with creamed leeks when you next have guests over. It looks like something you'd find in a restaurant, but this dish is ready in just 20 minutes.

700g new potatoes, halved or quartered if large

Calorie controlled cooking spray

4 x 125g pork loin chops, fat trimmed

1 large garlic clove, crushed with the back of a spoon

3 large leeks, trimmed and thinly sliced

1 tablespoon wholegrain mustard

2 teaspoons Dijon mustard

200g half-fat crème fraîche

Finely grated zest of ½ lemon, plus wedges to serve

Small handful fresh flat-leaf parsley, roughly chopped, plus extra to serve

1   Cook the potatoes in a large pan of boiling water for 12-15 minutes, or until just tender, then drain and set aside.

2   Meanwhile, mist a large pan with cooking spray and set over a medium heat. Add the pork chops and garlic clove and cook for 3 minutes, then turn the pork chops over and cook for a further 2 minutes until golden and cooked through. Transfer to a plate, loosely cover with kitchen foil and set aside.

3   Mist the pan with more cooking spray, add the leeks and cook over a medium heat for 4-5 minutes until softened, then stir in both mustards, the crème fraîche and the lemon zest. Season to taste, then bring the mixture to a simmer. Stir in the parsley, then remove from the heat.

4   Scatter the extra parsley over the pork chops and serve with the leeks, new potatoes and lemon wedges.

 SmartPoints value per serving

Butterflied chicken with a lemon, caper & shallot sauce

serves 4   prep time 10 minutes   cook time 20 minutes

The beauty of cooking with ZeroPoint ingredients is that you can splash out a little with the extras – like this buttery, French-style lemon, caper and shallot sauce.

4 x 125g skinless chicken breast fillets
Calorie controlled cooking spray
45g slightly salted butter
2 banana shallots, thinly sliced
2 tablespoons capers, drained, rinsed and roughly chopped
1 tablespoon lemon juice, plus lemon wedges, to serve
2 x 300g packs cauliflower 'rice'
80g watercress
½ red onion, thinly sliced

1   To butterfly the chicken, put each fillet on a cutting board and slice lengthways from the thin side, taking care not to cut all the way through. Open out the fillet, cover with clingfilm and bash with a rolling pin to flatten. Season and set aside.

2   Mist a very large nonstick frying pan with cooking spray and set over a medium heat. Add the chicken and pan fry for 4-5 minutes on each side. Transfer to a plate and cover loosely with foil.

3   Melt the butter in the pan, then add the shallots and fry for 4-5 minutes, until softened. Stir in the capers and lemon juice, then season to taste and set aside.

4   Meanwhile, microwave the cauliflower 'rice' to pack instructions, and combine the watercress, red onion and lemon juice in a bowl.

5   Serve the pan-fried chicken on a bed of cauliflower 'rice' with the sauce spooned over the top and the salad and lemon wedges on the side.

Cook's tip
You can use skinless turkey breast fillet portions for the same SmartPoints.

4   SmartPoints value per serving

Omelettes

Everyone should have a reliable omelette recipe they can turn to when short on time. These four new ways work brilliantly at any time of day, and at any time of year.

Chinese prawn

makes 1
prep time 10 minutes cook time 10 minutes

In a jug, whisk together 170ml hot **chicken stock** made with ½ stock cube, and 1 tablespoon each of **oyster sauce**, **dark soy sauce** and **mirin**. Put 2 teaspoons **cornflour** in a small bowl and stir in enough of the sauce mixture to form a smooth paste. Mix the paste into the sauce mixture, then pour it into a small pan. Bring to a simmer and cook for 1-2 minutes, until thickened and slightly reduced. Meanwhile, mist a nonstick frying pan with **calorie controlled cooking spray** and stir-fry 100g peeled, deveined and butterflied **raw king prawns** for 2 minutes over a medium heat. Pour over 2 large lightly beaten **eggs** and cook for 3-4 minutes, swirling the pan occasionally, until the prawns are cooked through and the eggs set. Slide the omelette onto a plate, spoon over the sauce and serve garnished with 2 trimmed and shredded **spring onions**, a 2cm piece **fresh ginger**, cut into matchsticks, and **freshly ground black pepper**.

5 SmartPoints value per omelette

Mushroom & spinach

makes 1
prep time 5 minutes
cook time 10 minutes

Mist a nonstick frying pan with **calorie controlled cooking spray** and cook 75g sliced **chestnut mushrooms** over a medium heat for 4-5 minutes until softened. Add 1 small crushed **garlic clove** and 25g **young leaf spinach** and cook, stirring, until the spinach has wilted, then stir in 1 tablespoon chopped **fresh tarragon** and 1 teaspoon **wholegrain mustard**. Season and transfer to a small bowl. Wipe the pan clean. Lightly whisk 2 large **eggs** and 20ml **semi-skimmed milk** together in a small bowl. Mist the pan with more cooking spray and return to the heat, then pour in the egg mixture and tilt the pan so the base is covered. Leave for a minute to allow the eggs to set, then push the cooked edges into the centre using a spatula, letting any uncooked egg run into the gaps. Repeat until the omelette is almost fully set. Top one side with the mushroom and spinach mixture, then fold the omelette over the toppings and cook for another minute. Serve with **mixed salad leaves** and **freshly ground black pepper**.

1 SmartPoints value per omelette

Ham, mozzarella & artichoke

makes 1
prep time 5 minutes cook time 10 minutes

Lightly whisk 2 large **eggs** and 20ml **semi-skimmed milk** together in a small bowl. Mist a nonstick frying pan with **calorie controlled cooking spray** and set over a medium heat. Pour in the egg mixture and tilt the pan so the base is covered. Leave for a minute to allow the eggs to set, then push the cooked edges into the centre using a spatula, letting any uncooked egg run into the gaps. Repeat until the omelette is almost fully set. Top one side of the omelette with 30g roughly torn **honey roast ham**, 40g drained and sliced tinned **artichoke hearts in water**, 25g torn **light mozzarella** and 1 tablespoon chopped fresh **flat-leaf parsley**. Fold the omelette over the toppings and cook for a further 2 minutes until the cheese has melted. Slide onto a plate, scatter over more chopped parsley and serve with **mixed salad leaves** and **freshly ground black pepper**.

2 SmartPoints value per omelette

Red pepper & feta

makes 1
prep time 5 minutes
cook time 10 minutes

Mist a nonstick frying pan with **calorie controlled cooking spray** and fry 1 small deseeded, sliced **red pepper** over a medium heat for 4-5 minutes until soft. Add 1 crushed **garlic clove** and 1 teaspoon **sweet smoked paprika** and cook for another minute. Transfer to a bowl and set aside. Wipe the pan clean. Lightly whisk 2 large **eggs** and 20ml **semi-skimmed milk** together in a small bowl. Mist the pan with more cooking spray and return to the heat, then pour in the egg mixture and tilt the pan so the base is covered. Leave for a minute to allow the eggs to set, then push the cooked edges into the centre using a spatula, letting any uncooked egg run into the gaps. Repeat until the omelette is almost fully set. Top one side with the peppers, 40g crumbled **light feta** and ½ tablespoon chopped **fresh mint**, then fold the omelette over the toppings and cook for 2 minutes. Season with **freshly ground black pepper** and serve garnished with extra paprika and mint.

2 SmartPoints value per omelette

Quick bakes & grills

Tuna, herb & lemon traybake

serves 4   **prep time 5 minutes**   **cook time 25 minutes**

Traybakes are the ultimate hands-off supper – just pop all your ingredients onto the tray, and let your oven do the rest.

600g baby new potatoes, cut into 1cm cubes
1 tablespoon olive oil
1 teaspoon dried thyme
1 teaspoon dried oregano
4 x 120g tuna steaks
2 lemons, 1 zested and 1 finely sliced
2 tablespoons finely grated Parmesan
100g rocket
20 cherry tomatoes, halved
Handful fresh basil leaves, to serve

FOR THE SALAD DRESSING
1 tablespoon olive oil
Juice 1 lemon
1 teaspoon Dijon mustard

1   Preheat the oven to 220°C, fan 200°C, gas mark 7. Put the potatoes in a bowl with half the oil and the dried herbs. Season and toss together to combine. Spread the potatoes out onto a large baking tray and bake for 15 minutes.

2   Meanwhile, put the tuna steaks into the bowl with the lemon zest and remaining oil, then gently turn to coat the tuna. Once the potatoes have been in the oven for 15 minutes, scatter the Parmesan over the potatoes and toss together. Arrange the tuna steaks and lemon slices between the potatoes and bake for 10 minutes, turning the tuna halfway through.

3   Meanwhile, make the salad dressing. In a small jug, whisk the oil with the lemon juice, mustard and 1 tablespoon cold water. Put the rocket and tomatoes in a bowl and toss with the dressing.

4   Serve the tuna and potatoes garnished with the basil and some freshly ground black pepper, with the salad on the side.

   SmartPoints value per serving

Quick cottage pie

serves 4   prep time 10 minutes   cook time 20 minutes   freezable

How to get this tasty family favourite on the table in half an hour? By using a few clever cheat's ingredients, cooking it on the hob, and finishing it under the grill. Easy.

Calorie controlled cooking spray

500g extra-lean 5% fat beef mince

300g frozen soffritto mix (diced celery, carrot and onion)

15g plain flour

375ml beef stock, made with 1 stock cube

2 teaspoons Worcestershire sauce

2 x 400g packs ready-prepared mashed potato (we used by Sainsbury's mashed potato)

320g Tenderstem broccoli

1   Mist a 24cm ovenproof nonstick pan with cooking spray and brown the beef for 5 minutes over a medium-high heat, breaking up any lumps with a wooden spoon. Add the diced vegetables and cook for 5 minutes, stirring often.

2   Sprinkle the flour over the meat and vegetables, stirring to coat, then stir in the stock and Worcestershire sauce. Reduce the heat and simmer for 5 minutes until the sauce is thickened. Season to taste, then remove from the heat.

3   Meanwhile, preheat the grill to high. Cook the mashed potato in the microwave to pack instructions. Spoon the mash over the beef mixture and use a fork to level it and create a pattern. Season, then cook under the grill for 5 minutes until the potato is crisp and golden.

4   While the pie is grilling, steam the broccoli for 5 minutes, until tender. Serve with the cottage pie.

The cottage pie can be frozen in an airtight container for up to 3 months.

Cook's tip

For 1 extra SmartPoint per serving, scatter 80g WW Reduced Fat Grated Mature Cheese over the potato topping before putting it under the grill.

7   **SmartPoints value per serving**

Chorizo & halloumi bake with chickpea couscous

serves 4   prep time 10 minutes   cook time 20 minutes

An easy Mediterranean-inspired dish that's full of flavour thanks to smoky, spicy chorizo, salty halloumi and sweet red peppers.

3 red peppers, deseeded and thinly sliced

1 red onion, cut into wedges

1 lemon, thinly sliced

120g light halloumi, sliced

100g cooking chorizo, sliced

3 sprigs fresh thyme

½ tablespoon olive oil

½ tablespoon sweet smoked paprika

FOR THE CHICKPEA COUSCOUS

200g wholewheat couscous

400g tin chickpeas, drained and rinsed

300ml hot chicken stock, made with 1 stock cube

2 tablespoons finely chopped fresh mint

1 tablespoon finely chopped fresh flat-leaf parsley, plus extra to serve

Juice of ½ lemon

1   Preheat the oven to 220°C, fan 200°C, gas mark 7. Put the peppers, onion, lemon slices, halloumi, chorizo and thyme onto a large baking tray and toss with the oil and paprika. Season and bake for 20 minutes, turning halfway through.

2   Meanwhile, make the couscous. Put the couscous and chickpeas into a large heatproof bowl, pour over the hot stock, then cover with clingfilm and set aside for 5 minutes until the stock is absorbed. Fluff up the grains of couscous with a fork, season to taste, then stir in the herbs and lemon juice.

3   Divide the couscous between bowls, top with the traybake and serve garnished with the extra parsley.

11   **SmartPoints value per serving**

Creamy broccoli gnocchi bake

serves 4   prep time 5 minutes   cook time 25 minutes

Looking for comfort food, fast? Soft, fluffy gnocchi baked with broccoli in a cheesy, creamy sauce and served with a side of spinach is just the thing.

300g Tenderstem broccoli

500g fresh gnocchi

180g medium-fat soft cheese

2 garlic cloves, crushed

150ml hot vegetable stock, made with 1 stock cube

Small pinch ground nutmeg

Grated zest of ½ lemon

2 tablespoons grated vegetarian Italian-style hard cheese

Calorie controlled cooking spray

360g young leaf spinach

1   Preheat the oven to 200°C, fan 180°C, gas mark 6. Cook the broccoli and gnocchi for 2 minutes in a large pan of boiling water. Drain and put into a 1.5-litre baking dish.

2   In a bowl, combine the soft cheese, half the garlic and all of the stock, nutmeg and lemon zest. Pour the sauce over the broccoli and gnocchi and toss to combine, then scatter over the grated hard cheese. Bake for 20 minutes, until golden and bubbling.

3   Meanwhile, mist a large frying pan with cooking spray and set over a medium-high heat. Add the spinach, a handful at a time, and cook for 4-5 minutes until wilted. Season to taste, then stir in the remaining garlic and cook for a final 1 minute.

4   Serve the gnocchi bake with the spinach on the side.

  SmartPoints value per serving

Chicken & pesto pizza

makes 2   prep time 10 minutes   cook time 20 minutes

It can be tricky to make a pizza from scratch in next to no time at all.
But it can be done! The secret lies in our two-ingredient pizza dough.

180g 0% fat natural Greek yogurt

**180g self-raising flour, plus an extra
2 teaspoons for dusting**

100g passata

1 garlic clove, crushed

**2 tablespoons chopped fresh basil,
plus extra leaves to serve**

**2 x 120g cooked skinless chicken breast
fillets, roughly chopped**

80g light mozzarella, sliced

1 tablespoon reduced-fat green pesto

Mixed salad leaves, to serve

1 Preheat the oven to 220°C, fan 200°C, gas mark 7 and line 2 baking trays with baking paper.

2 Put the yogurt and flour in a mixing bowl and season well. Mix together until a soft dough forms (see Cook's tip). Dust a work surface with the extra flour, then divide the dough into two pieces and roll out each to a 22cm circle and put onto the prepared baking trays. Bake for 15 minutes, until golden.

3 Meanwhile, mix together the passata, garlic and basil in a small bowl. Spread over the pizza bases and top with the chicken and mozzarella. Spoon over the pesto and bake for a further 5 minutes, until the chicken is warmed through and the cheese is melted.

4 Scatter over the basil, season with freshly ground black pepper, then serve with the salad on the side.

 SmartPoints value per pizza

Cook's tip
If the dough feels too
dry, simply add more
yogurt, 1 tablespoon
at a time, until you reach
the right consistency.

Cauliflower steak shawarma with green chutney sauce

serves 4   prep time 10 minutes   cook time 20 minutes

Tender spice-rubbed cauliflower, roasted and served with a quinoa salad and fresh green sauce, make this vegan, gluten-free dish a meal to remember.

Calorie controlled cooking spray

1 large cauliflower, trimmed and cut into 8 x 1cm-thick steaks

1½ tablespoons shawarma spice blend (see Cook's tip)

Grated zest and juice of ½ lemon, plus wedges to serve

240g quinoa

800ml hot vegetable stock, made with 2 stock cubes

400g tin chickpeas, drained and rinsed

½ small red onion, thinly sliced

1 tablespoon chopped fresh mint

2 tablespoons chopped fresh coriander, plus extra to serve

FOR THE GREEN CHUTNEY SAUCE

2 tablespoons chopped fresh mint

2 tablespoons chopped fresh coriander, plus extra to serve

1 garlic clove, crushed

75g prepared avocado, roughly chopped

Juice of ½ lime

½ tablespoon agave syrup

1 Preheat the oven to 220°C, fan 200°C, gas mark 7. Mist a large nonstick baking tray and the cauliflower steaks with cooking spray. In a small bowl, mix the shawarma spice blend with the lemon zest and rub the mixture into both sides of the cauliflower steaks. Put the cauliflower in a single layer on the baking tray and bake for 20 minutes, turning halfway through.

2 Meanwhile, put the quinoa and vegetable stock into a pan and bring to the boil over a medium heat. Reduce to a simmer and cook for 10 minutes until all the liquid has been absorbed and the quinoa is tender. Season to taste and stir through the chickpeas, onion, herbs and lemon juice.

3 While the quinoa and cauliflower are cooking, make the chutney sauce. Put all the ingredients in a mini food processor, add 2 tablespoons cold water and blitz until smooth.

4 Divide the quinoa between plates, top with the cauliflower steaks and spoon over the chutney sauce. Scatter over the extra coriander and serve with the lemon wedges.

8   **SmartPoints value per serving**

Cook's tip

If you can't find shawarma spice blend, you can substitute it with 1 teaspoon each of ground cinnamon, cumin, coriander and sumac.

Cod puttanesca parcels with herby rice

serves 4   **prep time 15 minutes**   **cook time 15 minutes**

Cooking food in paper – *en papillote* – is a fab quick-meal hack. The steamy parcel eliminates the need for oil, allows flavours to meld and creates its own sauce. And there's less washing up!

400g tin chopped tomatoes

1 garlic clove, crushed

60g pitted black olives in brine, drained and halved

1 tablespoon capers, drained and rinsed

2 teaspoons chilli flakes

2 teaspoons dried oregano

300g fine green beans

4 x 125g skinless cod fillets

2 x 250g pouches microwave long-grain and wild rice

2 tablespoons finely chopped fresh flat-leaf parsley, plus extra to serve

1   Preheat the oven to 200°C, fan 180°C, gas mark 6. Cut 4 pieces of baking paper into rectangles measuring approximately 30cm x 40cm.

2   In a small bowl, mix together the tomatoes, garlic, olives, capers, chilli and oregano, then set aside.

3   Divide the green beans between the baking paper rectangles, spoon over half of the tomato mixture, then top with the cod and the remaining tomato mixture. Bring the edges of the paper up and over the filling and double fold to seal the parcel. Put the parcels on a baking tray and bake for 15 minutes.

4   Meanwhile, cook the rice to pack instructions, then transfer to a bowl and stir in the parsley. Season to taste.

5   Serve the fish parcels and rice garnished with the extra parsley.

 SmartPoints value per serving

Baked potatoes with charred corn salsa

serves 4   prep time 5 minutes   cook time 25 minutes

An ideal jacket potato dinner for the warmer months of the year. You could also use the charred corn salsa as a taco filler, or serve it as a side at a barbecue.

4 x 180g baking potatoes
Calorie controlled cooking spray
2 corn on the cob
100g cherry tomatoes, chopped
85g prepared, just-ripe avocado, diced
Juice of ½ lime
Handful fresh coriander, chopped
100g WW Reduced Fat Grated Mature Cheese
120g 0% fat natural Greek yogurt

1   Preheat the oven to 220°C, fan 200°C, gas mark 7. Prick the potatoes all over with a fork, put on a microwave-safe plate and microwave on high for 3½ minutes. Turn the potatoes and microwave for a further 3½ minutes. Transfer the potatoes to a baking sheet and mist all over with cooking spray. Season to taste and bake for 15 minutes until cooked through.

2   Meanwhile, set a nonstick griddle over a high heat. Mist the corn with cooking spray and griddle for 10-12 minutes until they start to char. Set aside to cool slightly, then cut the kernels from the cob and toss with the tomatoes, avocado, lime juice and most of the coriander. Season to taste and set aside.

3   Split the jacket potatoes and fill with half the cheese. Serve topped with the corn salsa, yogurt and remaining coriander and cheese.

 SmartPoints value per serving

Parmesan-crusted cod

serves 4   **prep time 5 minutes**   **cook time 25 minutes**

A healthier take on the classic fish-and-chip supper – juicy cod loin fillets, topped with a zesty parmesan crumb and baked with thinly sliced new potatoes.

700g baby new potatoes, sliced

250g Tenderstem broccoli, trimmed

250g asparagus, trimmed and halved

Calorie controlled cooking spray

60g fresh white breadcrumbs

Grated zest of ½ lemon, plus wedges to serve

2 tablespoons finely grated Parmesan

1½ tablespoons olive oil

60g half-fat crème fraîche

4 x 125g cod loin fillets

1   Preheat the oven to 220°C, fan 200°C, gas mark 7. Put the potatoes, broccoli and asparagus onto a large baking tray and mist with cooking spray. Season, then roast for 5 minutes.

2   Combine the breadcrumbs, lemon zest, Parmesan and oil in a small bowl and set aside. Spread ½ tablespoon of the crème fraîche over each cod fillet then scatter over the breadcrumb mixture. Put the fish, crumb-side up, on the baking tray with the vegetables and roast for a further 20 minutes, until the fish is cooked through, the vegetables are tender and the crumb topping is golden.

3   Serve the fish and vegetables with the lemon wedges on the side.

9   **SmartPoints value per serving**

Cook's tip
Swap the broccoli for cauliflower or green beans for no extra SmartPoints.

Savoury tarts

It doesn't get easier than this – one sheet of ready-rolled puff pastry, four topping variations. Serve them for brunch, lunch or dinner with a simple side salad.

Salmon & spinach

serves 4
prep time 5 minutes cook time 20 minutes

Preheat the oven to 200°C, fan 180°C, gas mark 6. Unroll a 320g sheet of ready-rolled **light puff pastry** (keeping it on the baking paper) onto a large baking tray. Using a sharp knife, score a 2cm border all the way around the pastry. Brush the border with a little beaten **egg**, prick the base all over with a fork, and bake for 15 minutes until golden. Meanwhile, in a small bowl, mix 50g **half-fat crème fraîche** with 100g **0% fat natural Greek yogurt**, 2 teaspoons **creamed horseradish**, the juice of ½ **lemon** and 2 tablespoons chopped **fresh flat-leaf parsley**. Spread the mixture onto the pastry, then scatter over 40g **young leaf spinach** and 2 x 80g **cooked and flaked skinless salmon fillets**. Bake for 5 minutes then season with **freshly ground black pepper**, cut into quarters and serve with **rocket**.

 11   SmartPoints value per serving

Caramelised onion & thyme

serves 4
prep time 10 minutes
cook time 20 minutes

Preheat the oven to 200°C, fan 180°C, gas mark 6. Unroll a 320g sheet of ready-rolled **light puff pastry** (keeping it on the baking paper) onto a large baking tray. Using a sharp knife, score a 2cm border all the way around the pastry. Brush the border with beaten **egg**, prick the base all over with a fork, and bake for 10 minutes until lightly golden. Meanwhile, mist a large nonstick pan with **calorie controlled cooking spray** and fry 2 large thinly sliced **onions** over a medium-high heat for 10 minutes until soft – if the pan gets too dry, add a splash of water. Add ½ tablespoon **balsamic vinegar** and 3 tablespoons water and cook for 2 minutes. Blitz a 20g slice **WW Malted Danish Bread** in a mini food processor until you have breadcrumbs, then combine with 30g grated **vegetarian Italian-style hard cheese** and the stripped leaves from 3 sprigs **fresh thyme**. Spread the onions over the pastry base, then scatter over the breadcrumb mixture. Mist with **calorie controlled cooking spray**, then bake for 10 minutes until the breadcrumbs are golden. Cut into quarters and serve garnished with extra fresh thyme.

 11   SmartPoints value per serving

Bacon, egg & tomato

serves 4
prep time 5 minutes cook time 20 minutes

Preheat the oven to 200°C, fan 180°C, gas mark 6. Unroll a 320g sheet of ready-rolled **light puff pastry** (keeping it on the baking paper) onto a large baking tray. Using a sharp knife, score a 2cm border all the way around the pastry. Brush the border with beaten **egg**, prick the base all over with a fork, and bake for 10 minutes until lightly golden. Meanwhile, halve 200g **cherry tomatoes** and slice 4 **bacon medallions**. Spread 150ml **reduced-fat soured cream** over the pastry base and top with the tomatoes and bacon, leaving space for 4 **eggs**. Crack the eggs into the spaces, then bake for 10 minutes, until the egg whites are set and the yolks soft. Cut into quarters, season with **freshly ground black pepper** and serve garnished with chopped **fresh flat-leaf parsley**.

 12   SmartPoints value per serving

Chicken & asparagus

serves 4
prep time 10 minutes
cook time 20 minutes

Preheat the oven to 200°C, fan 180°C, gas mark 6. Unroll a 320g sheet of ready-rolled **light puff pastry** (keeping it on the baking paper) onto a large baking tray. Using a sharp knife, score a 2cm border all the way around the pastry. Brush the border with 1 beaten **egg** (reserving the leftover egg), prick the base all over with a fork, and bake for 10 minutes until lightly golden. Meanwhile, in a medium bowl, combine 100g **0% fat natural Greek yogurt** and 50g **half-fat crème fraîche** with the remaining beaten egg, then stir in 1½ tablespoons **wholegrain mustard**, 1½ tablespoons chopped **fresh tarragon**, and 120g sliced **cooked skinless chicken breast fillet**. Spoon the mixture onto the pastry base, then top with 150g fine **asparagus tips**. Bake for 10 minutes, then scatter over some more fresh tarragon and season with **freshly ground black pepper**. Cut into quarters and serve with **mixed salad leaves** on the side.

11   SmartPoints value per serving

Speedy pasta & rice

Chicken sausage & cabbage pappardelle

serves 4   prep time 10 minutes   cook time 15 minutes

You could use any type of pasta you like in this dish, but flat, wide ribbons of pappardelle look especially appetising. The name comes from an Italian word meaning 'gobble up'!

Calorie controlled cooking spray

340g Heck chicken Italia sausages, meat squeezed from the cases

300g Savoy cabbage, finely shredded

1 small onion, thinly sliced

250ml chicken stock, made with 1 stock cube

240g pappardelle

15g fresh flat-leaf parsley, roughly chopped

40g Parmesan, grated

1 Mist a large nonstick pan with cooking spray and cook the sausage meat over a medium-high heat for 5 minutes until browned, breaking up any larger lumps with a wooden spoon. Transfer to a bowl, cover, and set aside.

2 Mist the pan again, then cook the cabbage and onion for 2-3 minutes until just starting to soften. Season well, then add the stock and bring to a simmer. Cook, partially covered, for 3-4 minutes, until the vegetables are tender.

3 Meanwhile, cook the pappardelle in a large pan of boiling water to pack instructions. Drain, then add to the pan with the cabbage. Return the sausage meat to the pan and scatter over the parsley. Toss to combine, then serve garnished with the Parmesan.

 SmartPoints value per serving

Moroccan-style rice

serves 4   prep time 10 minutes   cook time 20 minutes

Inspired by the flavours of north Africa, this colourful one-pot recipe transforms turkey mince into something quite special.

500g turkey breast mince

1 onion, diced

2 tablespoons ras el hanout

400g tin chickpeas, drained and rinsed

225g basmati rice, rinsed

70g dried apricots, chopped

450ml chicken stock, made with 1 stock cube

Handful fresh flat-leaf parsley, roughly chopped

120g 0% fat natural Greek yogurt

100g pomegranate seeds

1 Put a nonstick pan over a medium-high heat, then add the turkey mince and onion, and cook for 5 minutes until the turkey is browned all over and the onion is soft. Add the ras el hanout and cook for a further minute, then stir in the chickpeas, rice and apricots.

2 Stir in the stock and bring to the boil. Reduce the heat, then cover, and simmer for 10 minutes until the liquid is absorbed and the rice is tender. Remove from the heat and let stand for 3 minutes.

3 Stir through half of the parsley and season to taste, then serve topped with the yogurt, pomegranate seeds and remaining parsley.

 8 **SmartPoints value per serving**

Cook's tip

For a more authentically Moroccan flavour, use the same quantity of lean 10% fat lamb mince instead of the turkey. The SmartPoints will be 14 per serving.

Seafood linguine

serves 4   prep time 5 minutes   cook time 10 minutes

Not only is seafood a ZeroPoint ingredient, but it's naturally quick to cook. This flash-in-the pan pasta dish, packed with prawns, squid and mussels, is ready in just 15 minutes.

350g linguine

Calorie controlled cooking spray

3 garlic cloves, thinly sliced

½ teaspoon chilli flakes

125ml vegetable stock, made with ½ stock cube

200g cherry tomatoes, halved

200g mixed seafood selection – we used a mix of mussels, king prawns and squid rings

10g fresh flat-leaf parsley, finely chopped

Lemon wedges, to serve

1 Cook the linguine in a large pan of boiling water to pack instructions, then drain, reserving about 150ml of the cooking water.

2 Meanwhile, mist a large, deep nonstick pan with cooking spray and cook the garlic and chilli over a medium heat for 1 minute until fragrant. Pour in the stock, then simmer for approximately 5 minutes, or until the liquid is reduced by half.

3 Add the tomatoes and cook for 2 minutes to soften, then add the seafood selection and continue to cook for 2 minutes or until heated through.

4 Add the pasta to the pan, along with some of the pasta water. Toss everything together, adding more water if needed until the pasta is coated in the sauce. Stir in half the parsley.

5 Divide the linguine between bowls, scatter over the remaining parsley and serve with the lemon wedges.

 SmartPoints value per serving

Mexican beef & rice casserole

serves 4   prep time 5 minutes   cook time 25 minutes

A brilliant all-in-one dish that's great for family dinners. Using frozen and tinned veg makes this a great standby if you're looking for a last-minute meal solution.

Calorie controlled cooking spray

500g lean 5% fat beef mince

1 small onion, diced

2 tablespoons fajita seasoning

225g basmati rice, rinsed

400g tin black beans, drained and rinsed

100g frozen sweetcorn

100g frozen chopped peppers

400g tin chopped tomatoes

400ml chicken stock, made with 1 stock cube

10g fresh coriander, roughly chopped

80g WW Reduced Fat Grated Mature Cheese

120g reduced-fat soured cream, to serve

Lime wedges, to serve

1   Mist a large, deep, nonstick pan with cooking spray and fry the beef and onion over a medium-high heat for 5 minutes, until the beef is browned all over and the onion is soft. Add the fajita seasoning and cook, stirring, for a further minute.

2   Stir in the rice, black beans, sweetcorn, peppers, tomatoes and stock. Season and bring to the boil. Reduce the heat and simmer, covered, for 10 minutes.

3   Remove from the heat, stir in half the coriander and scatter over the cheese. Cover and let stand for 3-5 minutes, until the cheese has melted.

4   Scatter over the remaining coriander and serve with the soured cream and lime wedges on the side.

12   **SmartPoints value per serving**

Cook's tip

Got some time on your hands? Whip up a quick salsa to go with this tasty meal. Combine 4 finely diced tomatoes with ½ small, finely diced onion, 1 finely chopped red chilli and the juice of 1 lime. The SmartPoints will remain the same.

One-pot mushroom & spinach pasta

serves 4   prep time 5 minutes   cook time 25 minutes

For speedy midweek meals, pasta is hard to beat. This veggie recipe is all made in the one pot, so there's minimal preparation and less washing up!

Calorie controlled cooking spray
1 small onion, thinly sliced
2 garlic cloves, finely chopped
250g mushrooms, sliced
1½ teaspoons dried thyme
240g wholewheat fusilli (or similar-shaped pasta)
900ml hot vegetable stock, made with 1 stock cube
100g young leaf spinach
80g half-fat créme fraîche
40g vegetarian Italian-style hard cheese, grated

1   Mist a large, deep pan with cooking spray and cook the onion over a medium heat for 3-4 minutes until just softened. Add the garlic and cook for a further minute, then add the mushrooms and thyme, stirring to combine. Season to taste.

2   Add the fusilli to the pan and pour over the stock. Bring to a simmer and cook for 18-20 minutes, stirring occasionally to ensure the pasta doesn't stick together. The pasta will be tender and the stock almost completely absorbed.

3   Add the spinach and stir until wilted, then stir in the crème fraîche and half the cheese. Season to taste and serve topped with the remaining cheese.

9   **SmartPoints value per serving**

Cook's tip
You could use any mushrooms you like in this pasta – try oyster or shiitake, or a mixture.

French onion spaghetti with goat's cheese

serves 4   **prep time 5 minutes**   **cook time 25 minutes**

Caramelised red onions, sharp balsamic vinegar and creamy goat's cheese are balanced perfectly in this spaghetti dish with a difference.

1½ tablespoons olive oil

350g prepared sliced red onions

1 teaspoon light brown soft sugar

1 tablespoon balsamic vinegar

150ml vegetable stock, made with ½ stock cube

320g spaghetti

15g fresh flat-leaf parsley, finely chopped

75g medium-fat soft goat's cheese

1 Heat the oil a large nonstick pan over a medium-low heat then add the onions and brown sugar and cook for 10 minutes, stirring frequently, until softened.

2 Add the vinegar, then add the stock, a splash at a time, cooking until the liquid is almost completely reduced before adding more – this should take about 3-4 minutes. Continue to cook for 10 minutes until the onions are softened and only a little liquid remains. Set aside a few onions, to garnish.

3 Meanwhile, cook the spaghetti to pack instructions. Drain, reserving 150ml of the pasta water, and add the cooked pasta to the pan with the onions. Add a little of the reserved pasta water to loosen the sauce and help coat the pasta, then season to taste and toss with the parsley to combine.

4 Divide between bowls, scatter over the reserved onions, crumble over the goat's cheese and serve.

Cook's tip
If you like, swap the goat's cheese for ricotta. The SmartPoints will be 11 per serving.

   SmartPoints value per serving

Pork tagliatelle with creamy white wine sauce

serves 4 **prep time 10 minutes** **cook time 20 minutes**

Succulent yet lean pork tenderloin fillet takes centre stage in this fuss-free and elegant dish. Ideal for an impromptu dinner party.

240g tagliatelle

400g lean pork tenderloin, fat trimmed, cut into thin strips

1 tablespoon olive oil

1 onion, thinly sliced

1 garlic clove, finely chopped

100ml dry white wine

100g half-fat crème fraîche

250ml vegetable stock, made with 1 stock cube

½ tablespoon wholegrain mustard

1 teaspoon clear honey

Large handful fresh flat-leaf parsley, roughly chopped

1 Cook the tagliatelle to pack instructions. Drain, reserving about 150ml of the cooking water.

2 Meanwhile, put the pork into a bowl with half the oil. Season, then toss together to combine. Set a large nonstick pan over a high heat and brown the pork, in batches, for 1 minute on each side. Transfer to a plate, then cover and set aside.

3 Add the remaining oil to the pan and fry the onion and garlic for 4-5 minutes until just softened, then pour in the wine and cook for 3 minutes until the liquid is reduced by half.

4 Stir in the crème fraîche and stock, followed by the mustard and honey. Return the pork and all its resting juices to the pan and simmer for 5 minutes, until the sauce has reduced and the pork is cooked through. Stir in half the parsley and season to taste.

5 Add the pasta to the pork and sauce and toss to combine, adding some of the reserved pasta water if needed to loosen the sauce. Divide between bowls and serve garnished with the remaining parsley and seasoned with freshly ground black pepper.

Cook's tip
When cooking with wine, you could buy a mini bottle, rather than a full-size one.

12 SmartPoints value per serving

Simple tomato & basil risotto

serves 4   **prep time 5 minutes**   **cook time 25 minutes**   **freezable**

Risotto always makes a satisfying and delicious meal, and it's so easy to make. This vegetarian version uses a passata-rich stock for a glorious red finish.

850ml hot vegetable stock, made with 1 stock cube

400g passata

Calorie controlled cooking spray

2 shallots, finely chopped

2 garlic cloves, finely chopped

250g Arborio rice

250g cherry tomatoes, halved

15g fresh basil, torn, plus extra leaves to garnish

40g vegetarian Italian-style hard cheese, grated

1   Combine the stock and passata in a large pan and bring to a simmer.

2   Meanwhile, mist another large nonstick pan with cooking spray and fry the shallots over a medium heat for 3-4 minutes until softened. Stir in the garlic and rice, and cook, stirring, for 1 minute.

3   Add the stock and passata mixture, 2 ladlefuls at a time, only adding more after the rice has absorbed the liquid. After 10 minutes of cooking time, add the cherry tomatoes to the risotto, then continue adding the stock until the rice is creamy and tender. This will take a further 20 minutes.

4   Stir in the basil and half the cheese. Season with freshly ground black pepper and serve garnished with the remaining cheese and the extra basil.

The risotto can be frozen in an airtight container for up to 3 months.

8   **SmartPoints value per serving**

Cook's tip
If you have time, add some chopped fresh red chilli or 60g sliced black olives to the finished dish. The SmartPoints will stay the same.

Spicy prawn pilau

serves 4 **prep time 5 minutes + standing** **cook time 20 minutes**

Using a curry paste instead of individual spices in this prawn and rice dish helps it come together extra quickly. The chilli, lime and coriander, meanwhile, give it a zingy freshness.

Calorie controlled cooking spray

1 onion, diced

2 tablespoons korma curry paste

1 large carrot, grated

250g basmati rice, rinsed

600ml hot vegetable stock, made with 1 stock cube

150g cooked and peeled prawns

150g frozen peas

Juice of ½ lime, plus wedges to serve

Large handful fresh coriander, roughly chopped

1 red chilli, deseeded and thinly sliced, to serve

1 Mist a large, deep pan with cooking spray and fry the onion and curry paste over a medium heat for 5 minutes until the onion has softened, adding a splash of water if the paste starts to stick.

2 Add the carrot and cook for a further minute, then add the rice, stir to combine, and cook for another minute.

3 Pour in the stock and bring to the boil. Reduce the heat, cover and simmer for 10 minutes. Stir in the prawns and peas, then cover and remove the pan from the heat. Let stand for 5 minutes, until the peas and prawns are heated through.

4 Stir in the lime juice and half the coriander, then season to taste. Divide between bowls, top with the remaining coriander and the sliced chilli then serve with the lime wedges on the side.

8 **SmartPoints value per serving**

Cook's tip
Serve the pilau with a half portion of the cucumber raita, p126, for no additional SmartPoints.

Turkey ragù with penne

serves 4   **prep time 5 minutes**   **cook time 25 minutes**   **freezable**

A Bolognese-style ragù always goes down a treat, and this quick-cook version using turkey mince is no exception. Why not make double and freeze some for another day?

Calorie controlled cooking spray
500g turkey breast mince
1 onion, finely chopped
2 cloves garlic, finely chopped
1 teaspoon fennel seeds
1 teaspoon dried oregano
100ml chicken stock, made with ½ stock cube
2 x 400g tins chopped tomatoes
3 fresh bay leaves
¼ teaspoon caster sugar
350g penne
1 tablespoon torn fresh basil, to serve

1   Mist a large nonstick pan with cooking spray and set over a medium-high heat. Add the turkey mince, onion, garlic, fennel seeds and oregano, and cook for 5 minutes until the mince is browned all over, breaking up any lumps with a wooden spoon.

2   Pour in the stock, bring to a simmer and cook for 5 minutes until the liquid is almost completely evaporated. Stir in the tomatoes, bay leaves and sugar, then simmer, covered, for 10 minutes. Remove the lid and cook for a further 5 minutes.

3   Meanwhile, cook the penne to pack instructions. Drain, then toss with the turkey ragù and serve garnished with the basil.

The ragù can be frozen in an airtight container for up to 3 months.

9   **SmartPoints value per serving**

Cook's tip
For a gluten-free meal, use red lentil pasta instead of wheat pasta for 7 SmartPoints per serving.

Pasta sauces

Pasta, sauce, bowl, fork – that's all you need for a meal in minutes. To serve 4, cook 250g pasta (for 6 SmartPoints per serving), then toss with one of these get-ahead sauces.

Spinach & walnut pesto
serves 4
prep time 5 minutes freezable

Put 75g **young leaf spinach**, 2 chopped **garlic cloves** and 30g **walnut halves** into a food processor and pulse to a coarse purée. Add 30g grated **vegetarian Italian-style hard cheese** and pulse until combined. With the motor running, gradually add 2 tablespoons **olive oil**, followed by 6-7 tablespoons water, adding it a tablespoonful at a time, until it's a pesto-like consistency. Season to taste, add ¼ teaspoon **ground nutmeg** and pulse again to combine, then serve with your choice of cooked pasta. The pesto can be frozen in an airtight container for up to 3 months.

  5 SmartPoints value per serving

Roasted red pepper
serves 4
prep time 5 minutes
cook time 5 minutes freezable

Mist a nonstick pan with **calorie controlled cooking spray** and fry 1 roughly chopped **red onion** and 2 crushed **garlic cloves** over a medium heat for 3-4 minutes until just softened and starting to colour. Stir in ¼ teaspoon **chilli flakes** and remove from the heat. Transfer the mixture to a food processor and add 3 **roasted red peppers** in brine (drained), 1 tablespoon **fresh thyme** leaves and 50ml water, then blitz. Season to taste, blitz again until smooth, then serve with your choice of cooked pasta. The sauce can be frozen in an airtight container for up to 3 months.

0 SmartPoints value per serving

Marinara
serves 4
prep time 5 minutes
cook time 25 minutes freezable

Melt 1 tablespoon **low-fat spread** in a large pan over a medium heat. Add 100g frozen diced **onion** and cook for 6-8 minutes until softened. Add 3 finely chopped **garlic cloves** and cook for a further minute until fragrant. Add a 400g tin chopped **tomatoes** to the pan along with 150ml water, then stir in 3 sprigs **fresh thyme**, ½ teaspoon **caster sugar** and ½ teaspoon **salt**. Bring to the boil, then reduce the heat and simmer for 15 minutes until reduced and thickened. Remove from the heat and stir in 2 tablespoons chopped **fresh basil**, then serve with your choice of cooked pasta. The sauce can be frozen in an airtight container for up to 3 months.

  1 SmartPoints value per serving

Alfredo-style
serves 4
prep time 5 minutes
cook time 5 minutes

Mist a nonstick pan with **calorie controlled cooking spray** and cook 2 finely chopped **garlic cloves** over a medium heat for 1-2 minutes until softened. Add 150ml **vegetable stock** (made with ½ stock cube), and bring to a gentle simmer. Gradually add 70g grated **vegetarian Italian-style hard cheese**, stirring well after each addition, until melted and combined. Remove from the heat and whisk in 200g **0% fat natural Greek yogurt**. Season to taste, then serve with your choice of cooked pasta.

  2 SmartPoints value per serving

Easy curries & stews

Coq au vin

serves 4   prep time 10 minutes   cook time 20 minutes   freezable

A super-speedy take on the classic French dish, this chicken and wine stew has all the flavour of the slow-cooked version. It's a great recipe to batch cook and freeze for another day.

Calorie controlled cooking spray

3 shallots, roughly chopped

4 smoked bacon medallions, roughly chopped

4 x 165g skinless chicken breast fillets, each cut into thirds

20g plain flour

187ml bottle red wine

250g chestnut mushrooms, halved

200ml hot chicken stock, made with 1 stock cube

1 tablespoon tomato purée

1 sprig fresh rosemary

800g Maris Piper potatoes, quartered

150ml semi-skimmed milk

15g low-fat spread

Handful fresh flat-leaf parsley, finely chopped, to serve

1   Mist a large, nonstick sauté pan with cooking spray and fry the shallots and bacon over a medium heat for 2-3 minutes, until starting to brown. Use a slotted spoon to transfer to a bowl, then cover and set aside.

2   Season the chicken and dust with the flour, shaking off any excess, then add to the pan and cook for 5 minutes until golden brown.

3   Add the wine, bring to the boil, then reduce the heat and simmer for 2 minutes until reduced. Stir in the mushrooms, stock and tomato purée, then add the rosemary. Return the shallots and bacon to the pan, stir to combine, then reduce the heat and cook, covered, for 10 minutes until the chicken is completely cooked through.

4   Meanwhile, cook the potatoes in a pan of boiling water for 10 minutes, then drain and mash with the milk and spread. Season to taste.

5   Season the coq au vin to taste, scatter over the parsley and serve with the mashed potato on the side.

The coq au vin can be frozen in an airtight container for up to 3 months.

9   SmartPoints value per serving

Mediterranean seafood stew

serves 4   prep time 5 minutes + thawing   cook time 20 minutes

This tasty dish could hardly be simpler, thanks to a frozen seafood mix that helps keep preparation to a minimum. The garlic toasts are an easy way to make it more satisfying.

Calorie controlled cooking spray

1 small onion, finely diced

2 garlic cloves, thinly sliced, plus 2 halved garlic cloves

1 teaspoon fennel seeds

¼ teaspoon chilli flakes

125ml dry white wine

400g tin chopped tomatoes

400ml hot fish stock, made with 1 stock cube

3 x 120g skinless cod fillets, cut into large chunks

300g pack frozen seafood mix, thawed to pack instructions

Handful fresh flat-leaf parsley, finely chopped

Pared zest of 1 lemon

200g ciabatta, cut into 8 equal slices

1 Mist a large, deep pan with cooking spray and cook the onion, sliced garlic, fennel seeds and chilli over a medium heat for 5 minutes until the onion starts to soften. Add the wine and bring to a boil, then cook for 5 minutes or until reduced.

2 Add the tomatoes and stock to the pan, season, then bring to the boil. Reduce the heat and simmer for 5 minutes, then add the fish and the seafood mix, and cook for another 3-4 minutes. Stir in the half of the parsley and lemon zest.

3 Meanwhile, make the garlic toasts. Set a large griddle pan over a high heat. Mist the ciabatta with cooking spray, then griddle for 1 minute on each side until golden. Remove from the pan and rub both sides with the halved garlic cloves.

4 Ladle the stew into bowls and scatter over the remaining parsley and lemon zest. Season with freshly ground black pepper then serve with the garlic toasts on the side.

 SmartPoints value per serving

Cook's tip
Serve each portion of stew with 1 teaspoon olive oil drizzled over, for an extra 2 SmartPoints per serving.

Nepalese keema-style curry

serves 4   prep time 10 minutes   cook time 20 minutes

An easy, mince curry based on a dish that's popular all over Nepal. It's traditionally made with pork mince, but you could use beef, turkey breast or veggie mince if you prefer.

1 small onion, roughly chopped

15g fresh ginger, roughly chopped

2 garlic cloves, roughly chopped

Calorie controlled cooking spray

1 teaspoon cumin seeds

1 tablespoon mild curry powder

1 teaspoon ground turmeric

500g extra-lean 5% fat pork mince

2 tomatoes, diced

Juice of 1 lime, plus wedges to serve

Handful fresh coriander, finely chopped

2 x 250g pouches microwave Thai jasmine rice, to serve

½ cucumber, cut into batons, to serve

1   Put the onion, ginger and garlic into a food processor and pulse until very finely chopped.

2   Mist a large, nonstick frying pan with cooking spray and cook the cumin seeds over a medium heat for 1 minute until fragrant. Add the onion mixture and fry for another 2 minutes, then stir in the curry powder and turmeric, and cook for another minute.

3   Add the mince and cook for 5 minutes until browned all over, breaking up any lumps with a wooden spoon. Stir in the tomatoes and cook for 10 minutes. Remove from the heat and stir through half the lime juice and all the coriander. Season to taste.

4   Meanwhile, cook the rice to pack instructions. Toss the cucumber with the remaining lime juice. Serve the curry with the rice and cucumber, with the lime wedges on the side.

10   SmartPoints value per serving

Cook's tip

Cooking with different mince? The SmartPoints will be 9 for extra-lean 5% fat beef mince, and 6 for turkey breast mince or Quorn mince.

Beef massaman curry

serves 4   prep time 10 minutes   cook time 20 minutes

Originally from Thailand, massaman curry is a fragrant, richly flavoured dish. Our version is flavoured with peanut butter and finished with a scattering of crunchy peanuts.

Calorie controlled cooking spray
350g lean beef stir-fry strips
1 onion, sliced
1 red pepper, deseeded and sliced
3 tablespoons massaman curry paste
250ml coconut milk alternative
250ml beef stock, made with 1 stock cube
2 teaspoons fish sauce
200g new potatoes, quartered
10g smooth peanut butter
2 x 250g pouches microwave Thai jasmine rice
10g unsalted peanuts, chopped, to serve
Handful fresh coriander, roughly chopped, to serve
1 red chilli, deseeded and sliced, to serve

1   Mist a large, nonstick pan with cooking spray and set over a medium heat. Add the beef, onion and pepper, and cook for 4-5 minutes, until the vegetables are beginning to soften and the beef is browned. Stir in the curry paste and cook for another 1-2 minutes.

2   Stir in the coconut milk alternative, stock and fish sauce, then add the new potatoes. Bring to a boil, then reduce the heat and cook, partially covered, for 10 minutes or until the potatoes are tender. Stir in the peanut butter until combined.

3   Meanwhile, cook the rice to pack instructions, then divide between bowls. Top with the curry and serve garnished with the peanuts, coriander and chilli.

   SmartPoints value per serving

Mixed mushroom curry

serves 4   prep time 10 minutes   cook time 15 minutes   freezable

The meaty texture of mushrooms makes them a great base for a veggie curry. We've served this ZeroPoint curry with naans, but you could enjoy it with rice if you prefer.

1 small onion, roughly chopped
15g fresh ginger, roughly chopped
2 garlic cloves, roughly chopped
Calorie controlled cooking spray
1½ tablespoons mild curry powder
350ml vegetable stock, made with 1 stock cube
600g mixed mushrooms
100g 0% fat natural Greek yogurt
10g fresh coriander, finely chopped

1 Put the onion, ginger and garlic in a food processor with 2½ tablespoons water and blitz to a smooth paste.

2 Mist a large, deep nonstick pan with cooking spray and cook the onion mixture over a medium heat for 2-3 minutes until fragrant and just starting to colour. Add the curry powder and cook for a further minute, stirring constantly.

3 Pour in the stock and stir to combine. Roughly chop or slice the mushrooms, leaving any smaller ones whole, and add them to the pan. Bring to a gentle simmer and cook for 10 minutes until the mushrooms are tender and the stock has reduced slightly.

4 Remove the curry from the heat and stir in half the yogurt and coriander. Season to taste and serve topped with the remaining yogurt and coriander.

0   SmartPoints value per serving

Cook's tip
Serve each portion with 2 x 50g mini naan breads, warmed to pack instructions. The SmartPoints will be 7 per serving.

Quick chicken korma

serves 4   prep time 10 minutes   cook time 20 minutes

Ready-made curry paste is a great time-saver in the kitchen, and you won't be sacrificing any of the flavour. This simple version of the popular chicken curry tastes amazing!

Calorie controlled cooking spray

640g skinless chicken breast fillets, diced

1 onion, roughly chopped

15g piece fresh ginger, roughly chopped

2 garlic cloves, chopped

1 cinnamon stick

4 cardamom pods, crushed

3 tablespoons korma curry paste

400ml chicken stock, made with 1 stock cube

40g ground almonds

2 teaspoons mango chutney

75g 0% fat natural Greek yogurt

200g green beans, trimmed

2 x 250g pouches microwave brown rice

20g toasted almond flakes, to serve

1   Mist a large, deep nonstick pan with cooking spray and set over a high heat. Season the chicken, then cook, stirring often, for 5 minutes until golden. Transfer to a plate, cover with kitchen foil and set aside.

2   Meanwhile, put the onion, ginger and garlic into a food processor with 2½ tablespoons water and blitz to a smooth paste. Add the onion mixture to the pan, along with the cinnamon and cardamom, and cook for 2-3 minutes until fragrant. Stir in the korma curry paste and cook for another 1 minute.

3   Add the stock and ground almonds, and whisk together until combined. Return the chicken and any resting juices to the pan, and simmer for 10 minutes, until the chicken is cooked through. Remove from the heat and stir through the chutney and yogurt until combined.

4   Meanwhile, cook the beans in a pan of boiling water for 4-5 minutes until tender. Cook the rice to pack instructions.

5   Serve the chicken on a bed of rice with the almond flakes scattered over and the green beans on the side.

Cook's tip
If you don't have a food processor, you could use ready-minced garlic and ginger, and grate the onion.

 10   **SmartPoints value per serving**

Golden tofu curry with rice noodles

serves 4   **prep time 5 minutes**   **cook time 25 minutes**

If you've never cooked with tofu before, this is a good recipe to start with. Bite-size cubes are simmered with butternut squash in a lighter laksa-style sauce that's hearty and fragrant.

2 shallots, roughly chopped

15g fresh ginger, roughly chopped

2 garlic cloves, roughly chopped

1 red chilli, roughly chopped

Handful fresh coriander, leaves and stalks separated

Calorie controlled cooking spray

1½ teaspoons ground turmeric

250g frozen prepared butternut squash

1 red pepper, deseeded and chopped

700ml hot vegetable stock, made with 1½ stock cubes

280g block firm tofu

150g baby chestnut mushrooms

400ml tin reduced-fat coconut milk

100g young leaf spinach

225g pack instant vermicelli rice noodles

1½ tablespoons light soy sauce

Juice of 1 lime, plus wedges to serve

1   Put the shallots, ginger, garlic, chilli and coriander stalks into a mini food processor with 2 tablespoons water and blitz to a smooth paste.

2   Mist a large nonstick pan with cooking spray and cook the paste with the turmeric, squash and red pepper for 3 minutes. Stir in the stock and bring to the boil. Reduce the heat and simmer, covered, for 10 minutes.

3   While the stock is simmering, drain the tofu and cut into 2cm pieces. Add to the pan along with the mushrooms and coconut milk, then cover and simmer for 5 minutes, until the mushrooms are tender. Stir in the spinach and noodles and cook for 2 minutes, until the spinach has wilted.

4   Stir in the soy sauce and lime juice, then season to taste. Ladle into bowls, scatter over the coriander leaves and serve with the lime wedges on the side.

11   **SmartPoints value per serving**

Cook's tip
To make this recipe gluten free, use tamari instead of soy sauce.

Indian-inspired turkey koftas

serves 4   prep time 10 minutes   cook time 20 minutes   freezable

Koftas are small, spicy egg-shaped meatballs and a different way of using mince. In this recipe, they're quickly fried to brown them, then poached in a tomato-based sauce.

1 small onion, chopped

2 garlic cloves, chopped

500g turkey breast mince

Handful fresh coriander, finely chopped

1 tablespoon medium curry powder

½ tablespoon vegetable oil

5g fresh ginger, grated

½ teaspoon cumin seeds

400g passata

2 x 250g pouches microwave brown rice

4 tablespoons fat-free natural yogurt, to serve

1   Put the onion and garlic in a food processor and pulse until very finely chopped. Put half of the mixture in a large bowl and add the turkey mince, half the coriander and the curry powder. Season, then use your hands to shape the mixture into 12 egg-shaped koftas.

2   Heat the oil in a large nonstick pan over a medium-high heat. Cook the koftas for 5 minutes, turning often, until well browned all over, then transfer to a plate, cover and set aside.

3   Add the remaining onion and garlic mixture to the pan, along with the ginger and cumin seeds. Cook, stirring, for 5 minutes, then stir in the passata and 150ml water. Bring to the boil, then reduce the heat and return the koftas to the pan. Simmer for 6-8 minutes until the koftas are cooked through and the sauce has thickened slightly.

4   Meanwhile, cook the rice to pack instructions. Serve with the koftas and sauce, topped with the yogurt and remaining coriander.

 SmartPoints value per serving

East African-style lentil stew

serves 4   **prep time 5 minutes**   **cook time 25 minutes**   **freezable**

African cuisine is becoming more and more popular in the UK. Spicy, lentil-based stews are found all over East Africa – our version is served on a baked sweet potato.

4 x 150g sweet potatoes

Calorie controlled cooking spray

1 small onion, finely chopped

2 garlic cloves, finely chopped

2 teaspoons Berbere spice mix (see Cook's tip)

200g dried red lentils, rinsed

700ml vegetable stock, made with 1 stock cube

1 tablespoon tomato purée

80g young leaf spinach

1   Preheat the oven to 200°C, fan 180°C, gas mark 6. Pierce the sweet potatoes all over with a fork, then microwave on high for 6 minutes, turning halfway through, until tender. Transfer to a baking tray, mist with cooking spray and season. Bake for 10-15 minutes until the skin is crisp.

2   Meanwhile, mist a large, deep nonstick frying pan with cooking spray and cook the onion, garlic and Berbere spice mix over a medium heat for 4-5 minutes until the onion has started to soften.

3   Add the lentils and stir to combine, then pour in the stock and tomato purée. Bring to the boil, then reduce the heat and cook for 10 minutes or until the lentils have softened and absorbed all the liquid. Stir through the spinach, then serve with the potatoes.

The lentil stew can be frozen in an airtight container for up to 3 months.

   SmartPoints value per serving

Cook's tip

Berbere is a fiery, Ethiopian chilli-based spice blend. You can find it in larger supermarkets. Or, for a milder dish, you could use ras el hanout instead.

Mussels with bacon & wine

serves 4   **prep time 15 minutes**   **cook time 15 minutes**

If you like mussels, you'll love this quick and easy dish that's flavoured with shallots, bacon, white wine and plenty of fresh parsley, and served with sourdough to mop up the juices.

1kg mussels

½ tablespoon olive oil

1 shallot, finely chopped

200g unsmoked bacon medallions, roughly chopped

2 garlic cloves, thinly sliced

100ml dry white wine

15g fresh flat-leaf parsley, roughly chopped

4 x 50g slices sourdough bread, to serve

1 Clean the mussels under running water, removing any beards. If any mussels are open, tap them lightly on your kitchen counter. If they stay open, discard them.

2 Put the oil in a large pan and fry the shallot and bacon over a medium heat for 2-3 minutes. Stir in the garlic and cook for a further minute.

3 Pour in the wine and simmer for 1 minute. Add the mussels, then cover and cook for 5 minutes or until the mussels have opened, shaking the pan every now and then. Discard any mussels that stay shut and, using a slotted spoon, transfer the remainder to a large bowl and cover to keep warm.

4 Bring the mussel cooking liquid to a gentle boil and cook for 2-3 minutes until slightly reduced. Turn off the heat, then stir in half the parsley. Return the mussels to the pan and season to taste. Scatter over the remaining parsley and serve with the bread on the side.

Cook's tip
Serve this with a mixed green salad on the side. The SmartPoints will remain the same

6   **SmartPoints value per serving**

Side dishes for curries

Want to make your curry just that little bit more special? Try serving it with one (or more!) of these quick, easy and flavoursome low SmartPoints side dishes.

Cucumber raita

serves 4
prep time 10 minutes
cook time 2 minutes

Toast 1 teaspoon **cumin seeds** in a small pan over a medium heat for 1-2 minutes until fragrant. Immediately remove from the heat and crush to a fine powder using a pestle and mortar. In a bowl, combine the ground cumin with 400g **fat-free natural yogurt**, ½ deseeded and coarsely grated **cucumber**, 15g finely chopped **fresh mint** and 1 tablespoon **lemon juice**. Season to taste and serve.

 0   **SmartPoints value per serving**

Quick pickled veg

serves 8
prep time 10 minutes + standing
cook time 5 minutes

Peel 1 large **carrot** and ½ **cucumber** into ribbons using a vegetable peeler, and thinly slice 1 small **red onion**. Pack the vegetables into a large Mason jar and set aside. Put 150ml **rice vinegar**, 1½ tablespoons **caster sugar** and 2 teaspoons **salt** into a pan with 250ml water. Set over a medium-low heat and bring to a gentle simmer. Cook for 2-3 minutes until the salt and sugar have dissolved, then pour the pickling liquid over the vegetables, making sure they are fully submerged. Seal the jar and set aside for about 15 minutes until the liquid comes to room temperature, then serve. The vegetables can be kept in the fridge for up to 2 weeks.

 1   **SmartPoints value per serving**

Spiced cabbage

serves 8
prep time 10 minutes
cook time 15 minutes

Heat ½ tablespoon **vegetable oil** in a large nonstick frying pan over a medium heat and fry 2 teaspoons **cumin seeds** for 1 minute until fragrant. Add 15g grated **fresh ginger** and cook for another minute. Stir in ½ teaspoon **chilli flakes** and ½ teaspoon **garam masala**, and cook for a further minute. Add 1 cored and finely shredded **white cabbage** (approximately 900g) and stir to combine. Cover, reduce the heat to low and cook for 10-12 minutes, stirring halfway through, until the cabbage is tender but still has some bite. Season to taste and serve. The cabbage can be frozen in an airtight container for up to 3 months.

 0   **SmartPoints value per serving**

Indian-style salsa

serves 4
prep time 15 minutes + standing
cook time 5 minutes

Toast 1 teaspoon **cumin seeds** in a small pan over a medium heat for 1-2 minutes until fragrant. Immediately remove from the heat and set aside in a small bowl. In a large bowl, combine 150g diced **cucumber**, 3 diced **tomatoes**, ½ finely chopped **red onion**, 1 deseeded and finely chopped **green chilli**, 5g finely chopped **fresh coriander**, 5g finely chopped **fresh mint** and the juice of ½ **lemon**. Stir in the toasted cumin seeds and season to taste. Leave to stand for 10 minutes before serving.

 0   **SmartPoints value per serving**

Recipe index

SmartPoints index